A LULLABY FOR MINNAH

Jah Smalls

jahsmalls

Published by SRB & Umisayspublishing

Copyright © 2025 All rights reserved

LOSANGELES, CALIFORNIA & Charlotte, North Carolina

Copyright © 2025

Formatted by Samuel Rain

Edited Jah Smalls & Samuel Rain

ISBN: 978-1-953234-03-2

All rights reserved by SRB & Umisayspublishing

No part of this book may be reproduced

or utilized in any form or by any means whatsoever, without

written permission from the publisher.

About the Author

Some days, I wrestle with ghosts I can't name, questions, heavy with "what ifs" and "maybe it was me." I wonder if my past has simply circled back, or if I just didn't pray hard enough before now. I know I'm not the only parent walking this path, I'm not the only one loving a child with special needs — but there are moments when it feels like the world has gone quiet, and it's just us. Just me, Tamica, and our baby girl, Minnah, holding on to each other in a kind of strength that words can never quite capture.

There are days when I feel like I'm losing a fight I was never trained for — but then she smiles. And just like that, I smile back. Every single time. It's not a choice; it's a reflex. Her joy breaks through every wall I build to protect myself from my fears. These tears of mine, they've become almost sacred — they baptize me in truth and remind me that love this deep will always command you to surrender.

The quiet moments are the hardest. The naps on the sofa, the showers that last too long, the baths where the water hides what the heart can't. That's where the battle happens — in the stillness, when the weight of it all asks my body to release every ounce of sadness it's been holding.

But even then — we fight. Even when the sky feels too heavy, we fight. Even when hope feels far away, we fight. Because love like this doesn't quit. It learns how to breathe underwater.

My wish — my prayer — is that everyone who reads these words finds strength in their own storms. That you keep discovering new ways to love, even when it hurts. That you remind yourself, again and again, that being a warrior and a comforter is the highest calling there is.

Kiss your superhero often. Tell them you love them — not because it's the right moment, but because every moment is. And to my daughter, Minnah Lyn-Simone Smalls — always remember, baby girl, you are loved beyond language. Always.

Introduction

For as long as I can remember, those we call "special" have walked the same earth, breathed the same air, and carried the same pulse of life as I. In grade school, I stood beside them—sometimes their shield, sometimes their friend—learning early the quiet language of compassion. I remember one boy in particular, a gentle soul bound to his wheelchair. His name slips from memory now, but not his spirit. My eldest daughter's heart once beat for him too; she prayed at his hospital bedside with the sincerity only a child can hold.

My nephew Nasir lives with autism. He resides in upstate New York, so I rarely see him, yet I'll never forget one visit when his hands found mine. Without words, he led me through his therapy exercises—his fingers guiding, his palms speaking a language deeper than sound. In that moment, I entered his world, and he, in his silence, welcomed me without hesitation. Sometimes I wonder if he knew what was to come—as if he were blessing my hands for the daughter who would one day arrive without words of her own.

Before my daughter's first birthday, I had written more than seventy poems for her. Each one was a seed of love, a whisper of hope. But when my laptop died, so did those pages—burned away like prayers in the wind.

I remember the grief vividly; it was as if language itself had abandoned me. Then came the signs, the stillness, the quiet truth—our baby, Minnah, would not speak.

To every parent and caregiver walking this path: I know the ache of solitude, the nights that seem endless, the days when love feels heavier than you imagined. We are not afforded the luxury of surrender. Our days unfold like riddles we are still learning to read.

This collection of poems is my testament—an offering of love without condition, patience without end. Within these pages live the echoes of what it means to care for superheroes disguised as children. Their strength is unseen, their beauty undeniable.

I hope my journey reminds you that love is not always loud. Sometimes it hums softly through the hands that feed, the eyes that watch, the hearts that endure.

In the end, we are each other's everything. And in the silence of their world, we discover the language of the unbelievably unseen.

The Movement

1. Oh Minnah
2. On This Day,
3. Mommy's Favorite
4. The Boodah
5. Night, Time
6. First Feature Away
7. Minnah's Solo
8. Nonverbal
9. A Smile Unseen
10. Haven't Kissed Your Smile
11. A Song Without Notes
12. Silent Love Song
13. In the Silence
14. Speak Bady Girl
15. I Wanna Hear Her Sing
16. S.O.S
17. Just Daddy
18. Daddies Don't Leave

19. Failure's Whisper
20. In Case I Break
21. Stay Home
22. Every Chamber
23. The Easy Part
24. The Quiet
25. You Are Love
26. Tomorrow
27. Her Quiet
28. The Weight of Her Wonder
29. Letter from a Soft Man
30. Brooklyn Prayers
31. Her Hands, My Tomorrow
32. Soundtrack
33. If God had a daughter

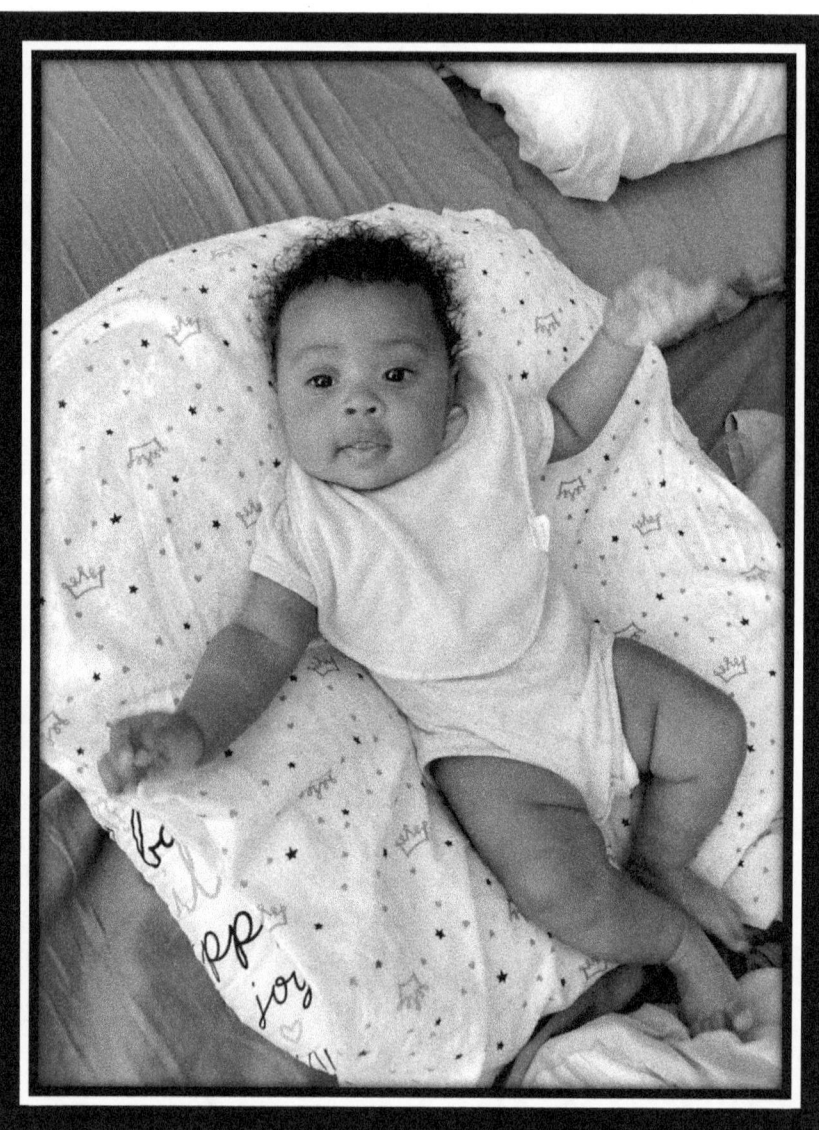

1. Oh' Minnah

My baby

    I am sorry for everything

loving you

isn't the issue

I am hurting because

I don't know how

    but I try with all of me

strolling down

    Am I Enough Blvd.

With a half-stride on

this can't be life Ave

I am crushed between buildings without bricks

dancing to everything I imagine you saying

    my baby

        My sweet baby Minnah

I'm sorry baby

    So sorry . . .

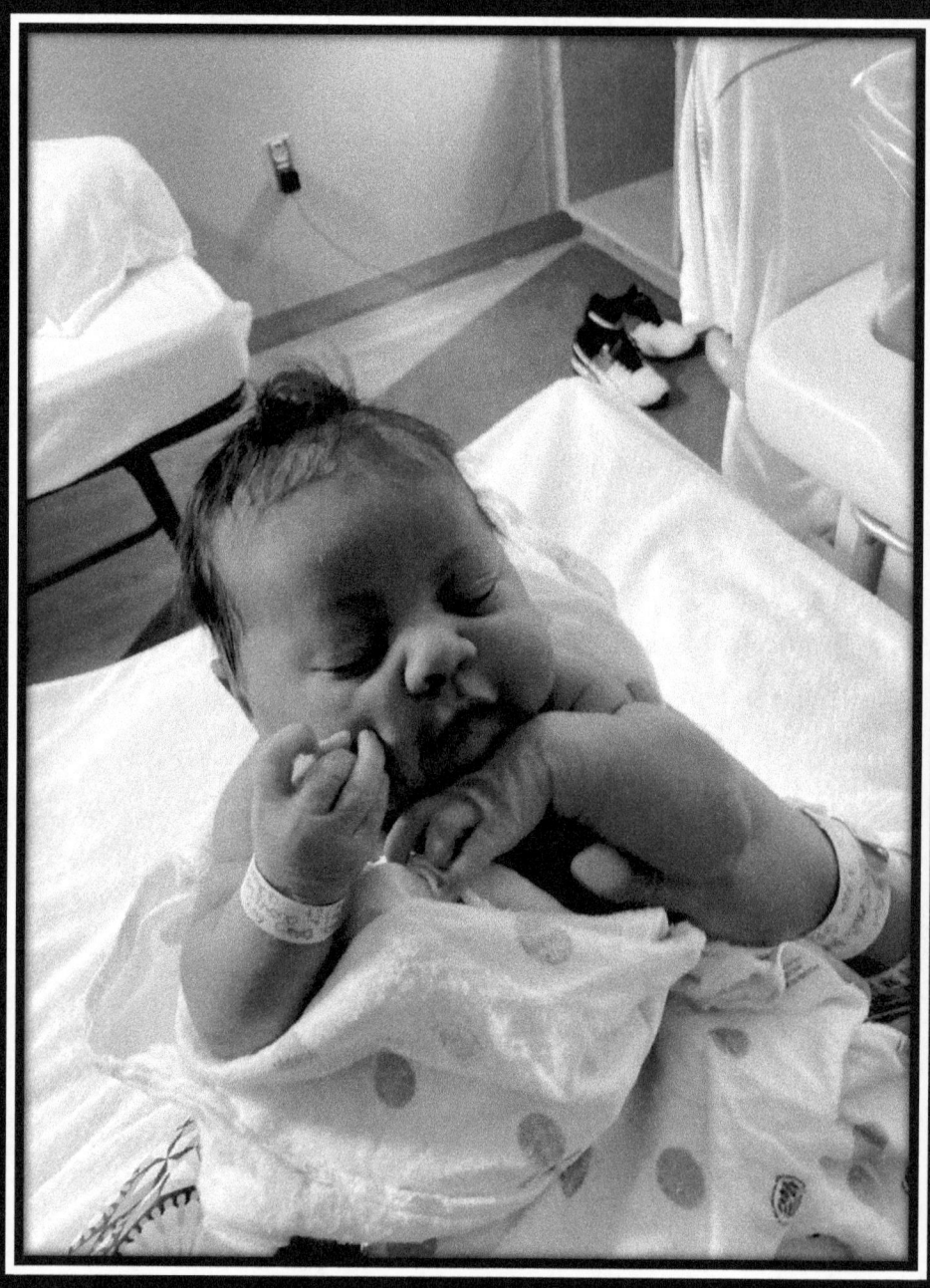

Your silence sings the lullabies my soul forgot to write.

Every blink you give rewrites my definition of love.

Your quiet breaks me open in all the right places.

I hear you, baby, without sound, you still shout grace.

You teach my heart the language of patience and wonder.

When you smile, heaven pauses to take notes.

Your eyes hold symphonies only God could conduct.

Every breath you take hums "Daddy, I'm here."

You are my favorite prayer answered in whispers.

The world calls it silence; I call it music divine.

Every heartbeat between us says more than words ever could

You teach me patience through wonder.

2. On This day

I plan to write to you always

both pen and paper matching every second breath

to say I love you in a dancing dawn

the hush of a swaying midnight

    I could name you love

in a world blessed to hold you

speaking in a million tongues

from Yoruba to Cherokee

lullabies and open thunder

every sigh in the solemn of softened souls

    I would wrap your hands in heartbeats

on this day

while mother earth beats her drum

and rivers rage because they can

in the silence of us I write you openly

in the holiest secrets

buried beneath the universe's fingerprint

3. Mommy's Favorite

And the first dance

hand swinging at purpose

this picture hued by one thousand words

we are seeing love

witnessing mom measure a melody of smiles

I remember you whole

the size of a fetus

heart of looming moonlight

filing us with laughter

one tear duct at a time

life growing in the love

our name

the salutations waiting to greet you

starting with your first dance

when we saw you

      then,

we Loved

4. The Boodah

I watch her every day

bend herself for you

arch her back into a bridge

preparing for your tomorrow

    that curve

a cradle and prayer

she builds balance with her discomfort

turns tired bones into a home

    for you

the glow in your chest

the beat in your belly

her hands are holy things

they shape you without sound

sing without voice

I watch her fall in love with you

in every thought

    every breath

Minnah, you are the hour's brightest light

the closing line to a perfect poem

love gathers itself around you

and happily, mentions your name

5. Night, Time

I whisper in the black, black night

soft throated

mouth closed

a prayer caught between silence and breath

I ask questions

I have no answers for

questions that tremble

questions that rise like smoke

I ask God

if He still speaks Hebrew

when He calls you,

my child—

if heaven bends low

to shape a language

that your silence can hold

and in that stillness

I feel it

the answer not in words

but in your eyes

in your breath

in the way you are carried

wrapped in His forever fingers

You, child of hush and wonder

teach me what tongues cannot

teach me how silence sings

teach me how questions

can be holy

And so, I whisper

in the black, black night

you are heard

you are known

you are loved

6. The First Feature

Perhaps

I should begin this poem

with a smile

one carved gently across the face

like morning light

stretching across the skin of still water

Or maybe

with a single teardrop

bearing your holy name

salt

making pilgrimage

down the ridge of my cheek

    Child

I couldn't believe

what I read that day

I saw your mother's hands

shaking

    typing

wet with wonder

and joy made of tears

she said

 guess what

she said

 there's a party

in my womb

Said

you heard my voice

and you danced

Oh, my soul

what music must've moved you?

what spirit stirred your tiny limbs

to stretch and swim

to lift a gesture as if to say

    that's my daddy

I didn't know you could feel me

didn't know one day of absence

would turn my voice

into a lifeline

but   it did

and you did

From the soft cocoon of creation

you heard me

In that hush they call

triple darkness

you were listening

and I

the second voice of your beginning

spoke

and the day unfolded

like scripture

like prophecy fulfilled

They say fathers don't feel

the way mothers do

but I say

fathers are doves too

we carry wings

and songs

and tears that make homes

in lullabies

    Child

I wept that day.

not with weakness

but with reverence

tears found me

standing proud

in the space between

manhood

and miracle

You

you brought light

back to a place

I didn't know was dim

You made me   father

again

7. Minnah's Solo

And then

your first dance

before your first breath

without sound

a hush of heaven falling to

the earth

we watched the beginning

imagined the future

from sonogram

to mommy's tears

your first dance

our first smile

8. Nonverbal

I whisper in the black night

closed mouth

soft prayers in silent breaths

answers are no shows

question crash against ceilings

maybe God speak Hebrew

whilst I pray in Arabic

how do I bend heaven

low enough to shape language

braid sound

twist a full sentence in your voice

my child

I see you, trying

inhaling what should become verb

and nouns

In the black night

I whisper loud enough

for you and I

Mom

and everyone who says

I love you

Dua in sun

and moon

when the sky cries

and with melting skin

in the black, black night

I whisper

when morning comes

I hear your

good morning

9. A Smile Unseen

My heart craves what eyes cannot touch
so, I pray you smile often
as bright as a winking horizon
dream of your first sun
the scent of the first rain to touch your skin
my child
I hope you smile often
cradled in the bible of imagination
I hope you dance in your dreams
mambo when our voices bring you rhythm
stretch you face in the spirit of love
though I cannot see your smile
it lives in the sky
tracing the clouds
lighting the stars
the icy colors of the extended universe
your smile
branded in a distant home

10. Haven't Kissed Your Smile

I felt you

long before the moon waltz in her belly

in the hush between prayers and pain

whispering poems for dollar signs

you ain't here

But I swear

I already know your laugh

the sunlight in its energy

that Sunday morning feel

I haven't kissed you yet

but I build its home daily

walled with lullabies and giant laughs

a ceiling of hope

with every corner longing the next moment

Baby girl

you haven't breathed earths dust

still, you live in my spine

the brawn in my fingers

The baseline that hugs every

        I love you like a prayer

no sun

rain

nor autumn's breeze, has brushed your earlobe

a first bath

camera flashes

Mom's selfies haven't married your eyes

I've yet to call God with

your fingers against mine

that first lullaby causing the

Curve in your cheeks

Oh, how I hope you dream

between colorful naps

and midnight restroom visits

Dear heart

when morning comes

open your arms so a forever love

will know your name

11. A song without notes

In this classroom I am the student

like free verse poetry absent a syllabus

a baby girl with eyes of dawn

parents searching for God's eardrum

I am a man in distress most days

even my white flag hangs half mast

seems I dream of words you're trying to find

Riding a sabbatical from voice box

to heaven's doorway

you speak in gestures

blink when time runs its course

Oh, the stories in your silence

when the world is loud

you gift us with great song

each step a new dance

Raised hand in a merciful pray

waving the patter of sound

again, absent of speech

I believe God made your language clear

every breath in love

as every breath plays

your music

12. Silent Love Song

My dearest Minnah
      this is my silent love song
I am afraid'   but still here
      confused and still yours
I am helpless hands
      becoming your bridge
crawl when you can   run if you must
      use them as a shelter
          they're ready when you need them
be it snow
      or triple digits in June
when your silence has run its course
      and your vocals remember their purpose
my heart will keep them warm
like earth rotating in waves
a brighter sun
and the moon dancing in darkness

Loving you has never been a question
      we're just waiting to hear an answer
          come from your lips . . .

I don't need words to hear her say Daddy, I feel it every time she smiles.

13. In the Silence

In the silence

thunder fails to rise in octaves

Our home

yes, our home

folds in upon itself

its temperatures strange

its warmth undone

Here, giggles forget to breathe

Here, laughter hides its face

The toys

those tiny prophets of joy

they turn away

they shun the fingers

that once brought them to life

And the silence

unyielding

sits heavy in the rooms,

a witness to all

that love struggles to restore

14. Speak, Baby Girl

Baby girl
I have watched you

whole galaxy in your gaze
sunrise tucked beneath your breath
and though the world listens for sound
I've learned your silence sings

Tell them
you are not the daughter of a wandering stone
but of a boulder
firm, unshaken
who carries the weight
of his people
and still finds time
to bend low and kiss the ground
where you crawl

You are his second self
his soft thunder
a blossom breaking through the first spring
summer-light spilling from your skin

Your voice, child

when it comes

will part oceans

Yes, some will be confused

Let them

You will lead with your knowing

You will teach

what the world thought

could never be unlearned

They say a woman comes from a rib

but I say

you came from love

from two trembling hearts

finding each other beneath

confused stars

Some believe in us.

some only believe in

judging what they never asked

let them scroll

let them type

let them assume

But you

you were carved from the cosmos

When the world says your name

they call on God

they summon women who prayed you here

They speak legacy

prophecy

a gospel yet unwritten

You, child, are a scripture

Tell them who your father is

tell them of the woman

who turned her womb into a temple

and fed you with hope

rituals baked into breakfast

songs that painted your dreams

Revolution lives on your tongue

and even in silence

your breath is defiance

your eyes, testimony

So fly, baby girl

soar

with or without a single sound

The world may not be ready for you

but you

you will make them ready and when you speak

when that first syllable escapes the vault of your lips

let it ring like a hymn

let it echo like your ancestors' laughter

let it teach them how to sing

even when the notes feel foreign

This world ain't ready for your glory

But it will learn

because you

sweet child

already know

your purpose

And I

your father

am already proud

15. I wanna hear her sing

The quiet doesn't match her eyes

on days when hope forgets her name

we mausoleum our home

fill our lungs of soul music

on those days the quiet reins

we fall under interpretation

our eyes become the victor

God's phone does not answer

I'll admit, it's hard

trying to stand in moving water

being a mountain with the weight of a pebble

there's no hiding

kneeling in love has bruised my knees

and still, we fight

we learn; we pray and teach

we're waiting to hear her SING

She's my daily reminder that miracles don't shout; they whisper, I'm here Daddy.

16. S.O.S

help exists in conversations

but never in our home

family

they're around for smiles

and fun time

but

these tears fall

on mommy's shoulders often

I am supposed to be the strongest

faith has abandoned me-

I believe I lost it

in a poem I cannot find

I often talk to God

and it's normal now

maybe

he does not like our conversation

17. Just Daddy

Full time screams

from a half pint shell

Daddy just ain't enough

Mommy still trying

to figure what's next

      and daddy just ain't enough

men are called the strongest ones

I now know I am still a boy

half a man on some days

barely a teen before curtain call

I love you

without caution tape or warning signs

wider than a dreaming galaxy

well beyond language barriers

through the trials seen and yet to come

      even if daddy just ain't enough

18. Daddies Don't Leave

Some men run

fade themselves in bottles

some ghost their own shadow

I am a different breed

with a wristwatch in my backpack

dishwasher by day

egg-flipper when the moment comes

I sling sandwiches and dilute her favorite juice

our hands match

foreheads trade kisses

and her fingers speak the language she cannot

she hones a handful of words

sometimes one will last us the day

bath times are a symphony

Screams pierce the ears

and warms the heart

the bubbles are life giving

the songs cradle our dreams

I am morning ready by nightfall

She's preparing the next great escape

some men, run

I back pedal

respect my sofa time

scoop whatever she gives

pray for everything she needs

I'm the broom pusher

emotional sponge

she's a cabinet cracker

pillow bouncing sandwich lover

together we spell team

forever we spell love

some men friendly door handles

finding new land against their boot heels

I forget the doors swings wide

hear her footsteps even when she's resting

her vocals haven't made their way from heaven

but her song dwells in an untouched sanctuary

holding a space

where love prepares its final exodus

some men are ok rolling against their heartbeat

my feet have never asked the question

19. Failure's Whisper

Every inch of my being

whispers failure

It's like praying to the sky

and watching it succumb to darkness

wanting answers feels like setting time on fire

God's language in Morse code

my mouth, a keyless prayer

I sit in a prison of my own ribs

cold and sheltered by lonely

starring in a whispering mirror

limits are your best

still not enough

broken would be an upgrade from useless

I fear what would be when she's grown

when my hands mimic my care

full of heart with no resolve

who will hold my baby

when my arms cannot hold themselves

Every challenge she faces, I face beside her, not as her hero but as her student

20. In Case I break

I am not the strongest man

So, praying and sweeping claim the

same space

some nights I hold my ear to your chest

attaching my hope to your heartbeat

yes, I crumble

when nightfall breaks my silence

folded in fetal posture I cry for strength

while riding a rocking horse of reality

I dare myself to dream

awaiting your first sentence

21. Stay Home

Men like me

don't get poems

medals of honor never claim our hands

we rock babies with our weary arms

match the rhythm of their heartbeats

with the magic of the moonlight

stand ovations require milk runs

favorite treats lead to big smiles

and yes, its tiresome

complaints and complements

collect the same pocket lint

so, we hug tighter

smile when eyes are fighting to stay open

time never on our side

pressure always calling our first name

my daughter wrestles storms inside her throat

carries an ocean in her chest

So, she doesn't speak

she turns our home into a question mark

and some days

we stand in the quiet long enough to find no answer

she screams

we sigh, she cries

and the room loses air

again, no trophy

giant hugs and a tiny nose tucked into my chest

men like me don't get poems

so, we find reminders in stanzas

tune our ears to hear everything our eyes remember

sometimes its happy

others a reminder

and no, we don't get poems

but we're always tasting love . . .

22. Every Chamber Open

With every chamber

open and without pause

teary eyes

and praying hands.

It's the everyday

that stirs me backwards

to same position

that worries all that I am

I am so afraid of tomorrow

      your tomorrow

what I see and what I do not know

the things that bond me

and control how I smile

Still, I hold you in that space

the core of my affections

      I love you in every moment

           I love you in Every Chamber

23. The Easy Part

Loving you
        Yeah, that's easy
Your silence
Is my battlefield
My chest
        A drum with no song
I don't mind being an instrument
it's just the braille keystrokes
the chord-less piano in your voice box
it's the struggle in the chakra
the wind that refuses the measure
it's the unseen matching what the ears can't hear
the guessing game
with doubt
it's loving everything even when there's nothing
and loving you through it all
but yeah
        that's the easy part

24. THE QUIET

In a home absent of voice

silence out sings thunder

bleeding eyes find space in the darkest rooms

where weary hearts pray for the toddler's words

seems her giggles hold her breath

so, she screams because

she can't say hi

    or yes

some days I fix breakfast with runny eyes

hiding the crimson color

from mommy's swollen heart

she prays so loud the room shakes

even when God doesn't answer

on those days music saves us

be it dancing or running around the dinner table

we defy the silence

sing against its audacity

I suppose we cry more than we breathe

hiding oceans in our back pockets

the sadness doesn't last long

morning sun comes without warning

the moon cat naps between warm milk

and   Disney plus

then the next prayer

for the next moment

focused eyes begging the eardrums

a little more patience

this silence reigns over the thunder

sits in the heavy of our home

glowing under a blanket of wonder

answers as absent as her abbreviations

but our love restores hope

Her laughter turns my fear into faith; her stillness teaches me peace

25. You Are Love

Fourteen weeks in heaven

stirring with a heavy hand

a distant voice

singing low country with Mississippi roots

    on this day Black america

    remembering a giant

ten toes on dignity drive

bruising the landscape of a new beginning

    "If I can help somebody"

washing the air with "Good Trouble"

incense burning

and white candles waving at the wicks

and   you the size of a memory

    Fourteen weeks

tucked safely in the core of a belly

cast away in an ocean of creation

    on this day

you become the only smile

God didn't give me a daughter to fix; he gave me a daughter to learn from.

26. Tomorrow

I believe in tomorrow

wrapped like sunrise in a silk vail

even though I can't see it

      Dear child

with your quiet mouth

teach me patience

with a steady heart

hum when you need to

scream if it helps you laugh

rhythm your warmth closer

these arms have your signature

like a swinging door here lays your freedom

      without worry

I'll be here waiting

and when your words are ready

I'll sing along to your favorite tune

27. Her Quiet

I look at myself every day

unable to bend sound to fit your voice

Singing so many things I wish you could say

but your silence speaks in lullabies I can't find in books

Maybe you're just having a moment to yourself

and Lord knows, I get that

The world gets loud sometimes

so loud it forgets how to listen

But I keep Hope in my back pocket

a prayer folded next to my driver's license

so when the angels decide to visit

they know

you're my only Wishlist

My final saving grace

folded in the same tears I'm holding back

You kiss my cheek all day long

from smile to tear drop

And though fear sometimes

wears my name like perfume

I know one day this earth will shatter

bend to the softness of your beautiful words

and we'll call that day Deliverance

28. The Weight of Her Wonder

You ain't said a word yet

but Babygirl, you speak galaxies

You talk in giggles and eyerolls

in Sunday morning stretches

and soft little sighs before you sleep

You don't need consonants or vowels to matter

you are the sentence that made me a man

the exclamation point God whispered into my lungs

I see heaven every time you blink

You make time jealous

how dare you stop the world

just to breathe on my chest

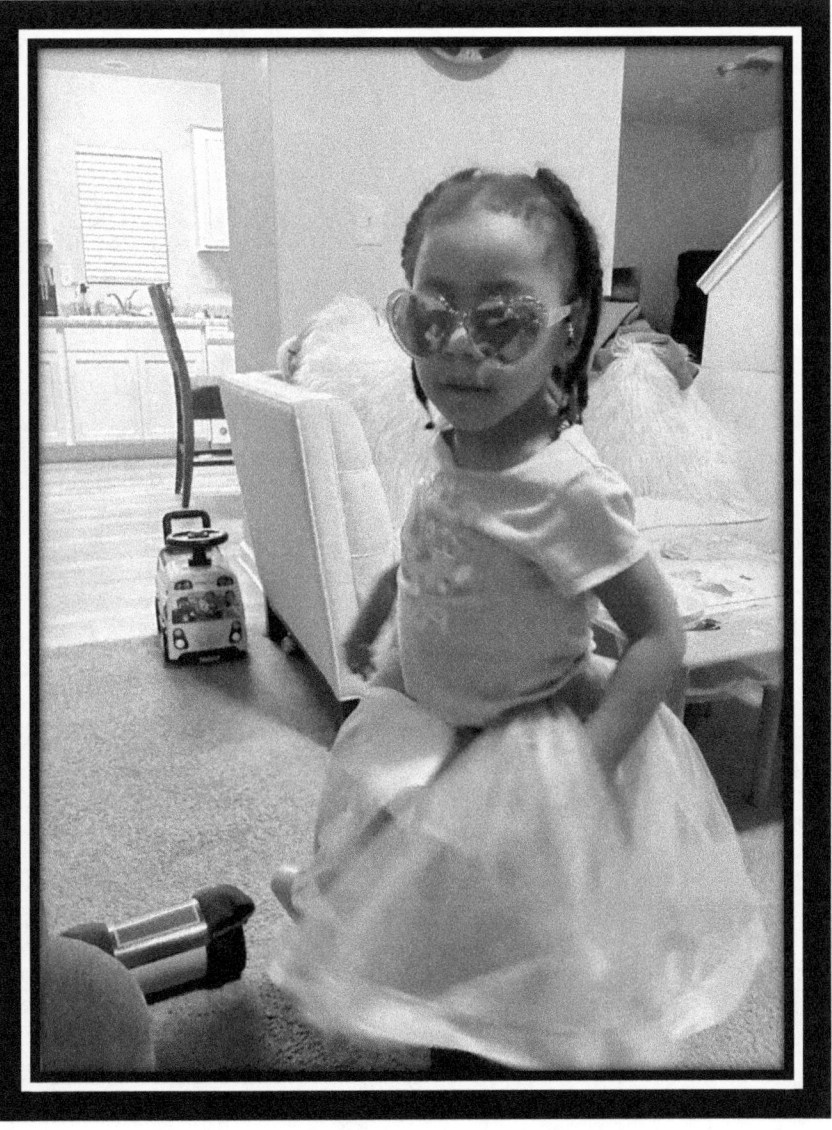

When she looks at me time stops, because love doesn't rush when it recognizes home

29. Letter from a Soft Man

They don't teach brothers
how to cry gracefully
how to turn silence into symphonies
how to pray over crayon drawings
and spilled juice like holy relics.

You're my teacher, my daughter,
my tomorrow in plated hair and rubber bands
when I hold you, I remember
gentleness is a strength too heavy
for some men to lift

So, I lift it for you
every day
with both arms trembling in love

30. Brooklyn Prayers

In Brooklyn,

we learned to talk through walls

Sirens as familiar as lullabies

horns filling outside like Sunday morning hymns

But your silence, baby

your silence cut through all that noise

You made me believe

in the kind of quiet that saves lives

So, when I whisper   goodnight

know that I'm really saying

thank you for finding me

She may not say much but she speaks directly to the father in my soul

31. Her Hands, My Tomorrow

You reach for everything

sunlight, cereal boxes

Mommy's favorite purse

the whole damn universe

And I let you

Because the world been taking from us too long

You deserve to grab something back

To touch joy like it owes you rent

So go 'head

wrap your small fingers around God's pulse

Show the angels how to hold on tight

Each day I spend with her, I understand a little more about heaven

32. Soundtrack

One day
you'll open your mouth and
drop a sunrise on me

And I'll cry ugly
like church mothers at testimony time
like Brooklyn stoops after rain

You'll say something simple
    like "Daddy
and the whole block will stop

Even the wind will' lean in like
Yo . . . you heard that?

    and I'll whisper back

I did. And I ain't never been the same

      after hearing

the soundtrack of her becoming

33. If God had a daughter

If God had a daughter
   she'd, be you
      a little messy
         a little magic
            a lot of meaning

She'd hum before she could talk,
   dance before she could walk
      and change a whole man's idea
         of what forever looks like

I see you
   and I see him smiling too
      probably saying

"See, that's what I meant when I created Love."

www.ingramcontent.com/pod-product-compliance
Lightning Source LLC
Chambersburg PA
CBHW031638160426
43196CB00006B/468